'Twas The Fight Before Christmas

'TWAS THE FIGHT BEFORE CHRISTMAS

A Parody

Josie Lloyd & Emlyn Rees
Illustrated by Gillian Johnson

CONSTABLE • LONDON

CONSTABLE

First published in Great Britain in 2016 by Constable

1 3 5 7 9 10 8 6 4 2

A CIP catalogue record for this book
is available from the British Library.

ISBN: 978-1-47212-511-8 (hardback)

Page design by Design23
Printed and bound in Italy by
L.E.G.O. SpA

Constable
An imprint of
Little, Brown Book Group
Carmelite House
50 Victoria Embankment
London EC4Y 0DZ

An Hachette UK Company
www.hachette.co.uk

www.littlebrown.co.uk

'Twas the fight before Christmas, when all through the house,
Not a creature was smiling, not even a mouse.

All the trouble had started that morning at five,
Only six hours before all our guests had arrived.

First Mum shouted at Daisy to vacuum the floor,
Before barking at Dad, 'Nail that wreath to that door!'

Tossing tinsel at Daisy to hang on the tree,
She chucked tangled-up tree lights at Sally and me.

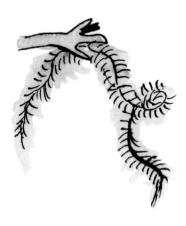

While her look of pure fear made it perfectly clear
That her internet shopping still hadn't got here.

Banning Instagram, Twitter, Snapchat and Facebook,
She pulled out the chargers, then started to cook.

'I'm fed up! You're all helping this year. Not just me.
We'll have such fun together. You just wait and see.'

When I burnt the mince pies, Mum started to frown.
Then the smoke alarm shrieked and the firemen came round.

When we tried to say sorry, Mum just shook her fist,
Sending Dad into town with an emergency list.

When the bell rang, we answered, 'Come in Uncle Bob!'
He was grubby and scruffy and started to sob:

'Happy Christmas? I think not. Your Aunt took the lot.
Both the kids and my pension. And, worse still, my yacht.'

Aunty Sue arrived next in a spanking new Porsche,
Telling Mum, 'Life's such fun since I got my divorce.'

Luke and Tara, our cousins, said, 'Move aside, dork.
Roll on New Year, when we're off to New York.'

While Mum's look of pure fear made it perfectly clear
That her internet shopping still hadn't got here.

Gran came next, clearly vexed,
and in need of a wee.
Grandad slumped on the sofa
    and yelled for his tea.

Techno beats told us Uncle Trev
and Pat were here.
Trev cranked up his music and
opened a beer.

Their twins fell out fighting,
before hurtling in.

'Stop it!' cried Pat. 'Now,
quick, fetch me a gin.'

Mum thought this Christmas we'd try
something new.

But Gran sniffed, 'That smells
foreign. Is it Cordon Blue?'

Aunty Pat began tutting and rolling her eyes.
'The twins won't eat veggies. Why can't they
have fries?'

Grandad slurped at the gravy
and spat, 'Too much salt.'

Uncle Trev dropped his glass,
grunting, 'That's not my fault.'

Soon a big fight erupted over what music to play.
The twins wanted Bieber, but Gran said Bublé.

We hadn't enough seats when we sat down to eat.
And no one ate Mum's poussin. (We'd filled up on sweets.)

Grandad farted loudly, but then blamed the poor dog.
Uncle Trev winked and proffered, 'The Yuletide log?!'

Tara sneered at Daisy, 'Your eyebrows are funny.'
Daisy retorted, 'But at least I'm not chubby.'

Mum said, 'Please, both stop it.' Aunty Sue said, 'Yes.'
The two teens stropped off, one east and one west.

While Mum's look of pure fear made it perfectly clear
That her internet shopping still hadn't got here.

When Uncle Trev claimed Christmas was only a fable,
Mum answered by saying, 'Fine. Let's clear the table!'

Scrabble was scrapped when Luke called Trev a 'turd'
  For claiming 'Aga-do' was a real five-letter word.

After Dad busted Grandad for
cheating at cards,

We all got together for a
game of charades.

I'd have happily swapped places with
that kid from *Home Alone*,

When Gran cackled, 'Joy of Sex',
instead of 'Game of Thrones'.

The remote for the TV then got broken because
Sally switched from *Die Hard* to *The Wizard of Oz*.

Cousin Tara filmed a Vine, then shared it online,
Showing Gran disco dancing after too much wine.

When Sue's new boyfriend rang, Uncle Bob
began to blub.
Mum nodded at Dad and pointed to the pub.

'To make Midnight Mass, Sue, you'd
better leave now,'
Mum said, flouncing out, muttering,
'Stuck up old cow.'

While her look of pure fear made it perfectly clear
That her internet shopping still hadn't got here.

She marched upstairs, kicking open the teens' door
Surveying the carnage – all that crap on the floor.

The dog was at the chocolates and licking off toppings.
Mum said, 'No more Pokemon. Hang up your stockings.'

Downstairs, Gran was snoring, her mouth lolling wide.
One twin chucked in popcorn; the other supplied.

'Leave out port and mince pies,' Mum told Sally and me.
'What, no whisky and carrots?' Aunt Pat disagreed.

Uncle Bob went rather white as
Tara read out her list.
'I agreed to an iPhone?
I must have been pissed.'

Luke yawned, 'It's a farce, who believes any more?'
Then the dog threw up chocolates all over the floor.

Gran began to choke. Sal yelled,
'Someone help her, quick!'
Gran spat out her dentures, thanks to
Bob's quick Heimlich.

Mum cried out, 'OK! Bedtime! It's
nearly midnight.'
'But it's snowing,' said Sal. 'Come on,
quick! Snowball fight!'

They all ran outside, knocking over a bin.
The neighbours' lights came on. The cats made a din.

In the snow on the windscreen of Aunty Sue's car,
Uncle Bob wrote, *I still love you, I'll never go far.*

All our neighbours charged out. Dad told them to, 'F off.'
Uncle Trev threw the first punch, then *Bish! Bash! Boff!*

'Hey, what's that?' I then asked, pointing up to the sky.
I stared up at a light zooming down from on high.

Over the roofs of the houses came a noise like a moan.
Was it a plane or a monster or an Amazon drone?

Snowballs hurled from the ground made the object swerve right
And flip over and down – all because of our fight.

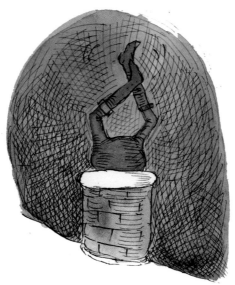

A loud screech, a yell and with sleigh bells all jingly,
The driver was launched head first into our chimney.

Luke helped me to clamber out onto the roof.
I'd always believed and now here was the proof!

I climbed up on board, and took the reins tightly,
Luke got in beside me, the sleigh rocking lightly.

'I'll lasso his boots,' Daisy called from above,
'But he's stuck really tight. So give him a shove.'

All the reindeer looked ready. Luke held out his phone.
'Great selfie,' he shouted, but Santa just groaned.

'Now, Dasher! Now, Dancer! Now, Prancer and Vixen!
On, Comet! On, Cupid! On, Donner and Blitzen!'

'Chuck down the rope!' Bob called from afar.
'I'll tie it round the bumper of Aunty Sue's car.'

We heaved and we ho'ed and then out he popped,
Tumbling down to the lawn and then everything stopped.

Uncle Trev said, 'Hey look!
It's that bloke from KFC.
The kids'll have a bucket, mate.
Chicken wings for me.'

Santa spoke: 'No more fighting
and let's pull together.
Or else, you'll be on my
naughty list… for ever.'

He sprinkled magic on the adults,
saying, 'There was no Santa here,'
Before telling us kids, 'I'll see you
next year.'

'Now excuse me I'm busy,' he said
with a wink,
And *whoosh!* he was up on the roof
in a blink.

Then what to our wondrous eyes should appear?
But the internet order! The last of the year!

'I'm late,' said the driver, 'but you'll find everything wrapped.'
Mum cried, 'Oh thank goodness'. Everyone clapped.

In the doorway, Dad stopped for a mistletoe kiss,
Telling Mum, 'Pucker up, you're my number one wish.'

Gran said, 'Who wants a nightcap? Make mine a sherry.'
'I'll do cocoa for the kids,' said Pat. 'Won't that be merry?'

And then I saw Santa on his sleigh in the sky.
He looked down and grinned and waved me goodbye.

And I heard him exclaim, ere he drove out of sight,
'Happy Christmas to all, and to all a goodnight!'

Josie Lloyd & Emlyn Rees are the bestselling authors of *Come Together*, *A Twist of Fate*, *Hunted* and many other novels. They're married and live in Brighton with their three children.

Gillian Johnson is a prize-winning writer and illustrator whose work has been translated into ten languages. She lives in Oxford with her husband and two sons.